...g with travellers a wealth of experience and a passion for travel.

Rely on Thomas Cook as your travelling companion on your next trip and benefit from our unique heritage.

Thomas Cook **pocket** guides

WARWICK

Your travelling companion since 1873

Written by Lisa Francesca Nand

Published by Thomas Cook Publishing
A division of Thomas Cook Tour Operations Limited
Company registration no. 3772199 England
The Thomas Cook Business Park, Unit 9, Coningsby Road,
Peterborough PE3 8SB, United Kingdom
Email: books@thomascook.com, Tel: +44 (0) 1733 416477
www.thomascookpublishing.com

Produced by Cambridge Publishing Management Limited
Burr Elm Court, Main Street, Caldecote CB23 7NU
www.cambridgepm.co.uk

ISBN: 978-1-84848-488-7

First edition © 2011 Thomas Cook Publishing
Text © Thomas Cook Publishing
Cartography supplied by Redmoor Design, Tavistock, Devon
Map data © OpenStreetMap contributors CC-BY-SA, www.openstreetmap.org,
www.creativecommons.org

Series Editor: Karen Beaulah
Production/DTP: Steven Collins

Printed and bound in Spain by GraphyCems

Cover photography © Latitudestock

CONTENTS

SYMBOLS KEY

The following symbols are used throughout this book:

a address **t** telephone **f** fax **w** website address **e** email
c opening times **N** public transport connections **!** important

The following symbols are used on the maps:

i	information office	■	point of interest
🛡	police station	O	city
🚌	bus station	O	large town
🚆	railway station	○	small town
✉	post office	=	motorway
1	numbers denote featured	—	main road
	cafés, restaurants	—	minor road
	& venues	—	railway

PRICE CATEGORIES

The ratings below indicate average price rates for a double
room per night, including breakfast:

£ under £70 ££ £70–120 £££ over £120

The typical cost for a three-course meal without drinks
is as follows:

£ under £15 ££ £15–25 £££ over £25

▶ *Warwick's spectacular fairytale castle*

INTRODUCING
Warwick

Introduction

As one might expect from a town that is centred around a fortress, Warwick has been the site of some fierce battles over the centuries. From humble beginnings, it has survived adversity, wars, plagues and almost total destruction by fire.

Beginning life as a small settlement next to the River Avon, strategically positioned on a small hill, by the 10th century Warwick had become a fortress with a wall and large ditch to deter potential invaders. The Normans built the first incarnation of the castle, initially of wood, and the Middle Ages saw the building of a bigger wall, two of whose gates still stand, and the further expansion of the now flourishing market town.

Despite frequent attacks, the settlement continued to flourish and, fortunately for today's visitor, the county town of Warwickshire sturdily withstood all the slings and arrows to become one of the UK's most visited destinations. Modern-day Warwick, with its long cultural and historic heritage, also boasts an increasing reputation for a lively café culture, independent shops and good restaurants. It is small but perfectly formed, and the picturesque streets of the town centre remain refreshingly unspoilt. It manages to retain a young and vibrant atmosphere, as well as being a haven for antiquities, tea shops and history.

Rising upwards and outwards from the Avon valley, the expansion of both Warwick and neighbouring Leamington Spa have meant the two towns now effectively form one conurbation, governed together under the umbrella of Warwick District Council.

Warwick is now known the world over for its castle, built on the orders of William the Conqueror in 1068. Dominating the city's landscape, and remaining one of the most complete medieval castles in the UK, **Warwick Castle** has moved with the times to become a thriving centre for modern-day performances and historical re-enactments.

The current-day draws of shopping, cafés, bars and international festivals firmly place Warwick in the 21st century, with modern attractions complementing a contemporary cultural focus on music and the arts. Stroll through Warwick's medieval streets, however, and you can still almost hear the cries of the craftsmen, brewers, bakers and blacksmiths echoing down the centuries.

◔ *Be charmed by the town's quaint medieval streets*

When to go

ANNUAL EVENTS

With a programme of events covering all year round, Warwick does not appear to have an off-peak season. The colder months are well catered for by the castle, in which it's possible to spend entire days, cosy and warm while being entertained by shows, taking tours of the medieval rooms, inspecting the dungeons, and attending banquets and Highwayman's Suppers. October sees the Mop Fair come to town, a tradition that dates back to the time of King Edward III, pre-dating even the market. From November onwards, Christmas events see the castle decorated in all its glory, playing host to a number of themed events, including the superb **Kingmakers Mediaeval Christmas Banquet** (see box page 52). The whole town dresses up for the celebrations of the **Victorian Evening**.

As the months start to warm up, the castle's outdoor attractions shine, with enchanting gardens to enjoy, birds-of-prey displays and jousting. It's a perfect time for picnicking in the grounds. Spring is also the perfect time to start enjoying the three large parks that surround the city. Guided town walks conducted by a well-informed local guide start on Sunday mornings from May to the end of September.

For sports fans **Warwick Racecourse**, with one of the oldest surviving grandstands in the country, retains a full racing calendar all year round, and there's cricket, starting in April and going on until September, at **Warwick Cricket Club**, whose members play in the Warwickshire Cricket League and who are always keen to have spectators. Further afield there's the county ground at Edgbaston for the bigger matches.

Summer sees the arrival of not one but two international festivals – the **Warwick International Festival** (ⓦ www.warwickintfestival.org) from June to July and the **Warwick Folk Festival** (ⓦ www.warwickfolkfestival.co.uk) in late July. The streets fill with visitors as the cafés spill on to the pavements and street performers entertain a keen crowd. In early October comes **Warwick Words**, Festival of Literature and Spoken Word (ⓦ www.warwickwords.co.uk), with an exciting programme of performances, talks, workshops, literary lunches and afternoon teas to keep you entertained.

◓ The castle's delightful grounds play host to a full calendar of events

History

Although a settlement existed in Roman times, the formidable Ethelfleda, 'Lady of the Mercians', created a fortified town, or *burh*, in the 10th century to deter the Vikings from attacking. A deep ditch and protective wall were built around the market town, which also boasted a mint. The year 1068 saw William the Conqueror instruct his Norman barons to construct a wooden castle and, by the time the Domesday Book was compiled in 1086, the town boasted 1,500 inhabitants. Warwick began to prosper.

By the Middle Ages a sturdier wall had been built, with great gates to the north, west and east. Today, Eastgate and Westgate still stand. The 12th and 13th centuries saw a flurry of worship, with the building of St Mary's Church, the founding of St Sepulchre's Priory and the arrival of the Dominican 'black friars', who ventured forth into the town to preach. Medieval times also saw the Earl of Warwick, known as the 'kingmaker' and one of the most famous men in England, occupy the castle. The town bustled with weekly markets, crafts-folk and commerce, hosting annual fairs that attracted traders from far and wide. By 1260 work started to replace the wooden castle with what would become the grand stone masterpiece you see today.

The early 17th-century population was dealt a blow with the death of many from plague. Disaster struck again in 1694 when thanks, as lore has it, to an incident involving a young boy, a thatched roof and a match, a fire raged through the city, destroying many of the town's buildings.

Warwick battled through wars, fires and disease, and by the late 18th century could lay claim to two significant canal routes. Streets were paved, gas and water supplies were introduced and, by 1852, the railways arrived. Despite this development, Warwick remained a market town, largely architecturally unscathed by industrial growth, and by the end of World War II still had a population of fewer than 15,000 people. As horse-drawn trams gave way to electric, trams to buses and trains, Warwick and Leamington Spa inched towards each other to create the lively conurbation that exists today.

● *Eastgate stands as a relic of Warwick's Norman past*

Culture

Warwick plays to its strengths with a strong emphasis on traditional English culture. Tea shops and Tudor houses abound, with a thriving air of nostalgia. Several excellent museums showcase the historical significance of Warwick as a military base, as well as its illustrious royal legacy. Look more closely, however, and you'll find a surprisingly modern, arty undercurrent with many independent cultural ventures and galleries. On a wider scale, the **Warwick Arts Centre** (see page 18) at the nearby University of Warwick is one of the largest of its kind in the UK. Despite being located away from the town centre, it has helped put Warwick on the world map for cutting-edge art, exhibitions and theatre.

Warwick is also on the world-event stage through its annual International Festival and Folk Festival and, with a penchant for independent bookshops, it also hosts an annual literary festival, Warwick Words. There are also frequent musical evenings and concerts, including those at the **Collegiate Church of St Mary** (see page 54).

Needless to say, **Warwick Castle** (see pages 42–53) takes centre stage in Warwick's cultural calendar, with year-round historical re-enactments, exhibitions focusing on social history and a range of banquets and suppers geared towards the historically curious visitor.

● *Medieval punishments and a spooky crypt lurk behind this grand façade*

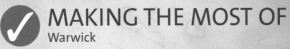

MAKING THE MOST OF
Warwick

Shopping

What to buy

The few chain stores there are in Warwick are tastefully enveloped within the town's Tudor and Georgian architectural tradition and there's a great deal more space and emphasis given to independent shops and boutiques than to international brands, with a distinct entrepreneurial spirit evident in some of the ventures. Souvenirs, clotted-cream fudge, chocolates and cakes are available everywhere, yet swish boutiques, innovative ideas and specialist shops are also in plentiful supply. There are numerous venues (including restaurant/gallery combinations) where you can buy original art, as well as plenty of card and gift shops. Warwick is also a fabulous place to find old English antiques, furnishings and bric-a-brac, ranging from the exclusive and elegant to everyday home decoration, crockery, glassware and brass.

Where to buy it

The best of the boutiques and independent shops are to be found on **Smith Street** (Warwick's oldest shopping street) and **Swan Street** (Warwick's busiest shopping street). Antique shops are dotted all over town, as are some great charity shops. Foodstuffs and speciality local produce can be found amid the tea rooms, with several incorporating shops selling jams, pickles and other home-made goods, and there is even a local brew shop at **The Slaughterhouse Brewery** on Bridge Street (☏ 01926 490986 Ⓦ www.slaughterhousebrewery.com).

The market

With a centuries-old reputation as a market town, Warwick's **Market Place** still hosts a traditional market every Saturday from 09.00 to 16.00 (except for two Saturdays in October when the funfair is in town). Although the market itself is small, it is big on atmosphere and, set amid the street tables of the pubs and cafés on the square, it has something of a Continental feel when weather permits. Here you'll find traditional market fare, fruit and vegetables and household goods, as well as home-made cakes, a flower stall, several clothes vendors and, invariably, a very popular French stall selling olives and nuts.

▲ *Fresh produce, plenty of atmosphere and many a bargain at the market*

Eating & drinking

The few chain coffee shops and restaurants in the centre have – as with the shops – been sensitively camouflaged within Tudor buildings and low-rise cottages. A whole host of international food – Italian, Indian, Thai, Chinese, Lebanese, Turkish and, of course, traditional English – is available. For daytime dining there are countless tea rooms and cafés to choose from, many housed in rickety or interesting buildings, and for lunch and evening a sophisticated array of options, including restaurant/ art gallery combinations and tasteful themes are on offer.

Warwick is also home to scores of traditional pubs, with one on almost every major street, and several gathered around Market Place. Most of these are cosy, wood panelled and oak beamed, with roaring fires adding to the atmosphere in the cooler months and surprisingly extensive beer gardens for warmer days.

The farmers' market takes place on the third Friday of every month in Swan Street, from 09.00 to 14.00, offering fresh local produce straight from the farmers. It's a great place to stock up on meats, eggs, pickles, chutneys, cheese, freshly baked breads, biscuits, cakes and pastries, as well as choosing from an assortment of wines and ciders.

A few delis also offer takeaway options, perfect for picnics, and there are plenty of places for seasonal alfresco dining, including **St Nicholas Park**, the riverside and **Priory Park**, as well as the beautiful **Pageant Garden** as you come out of the castle (see box page 30). Within the castle grounds are several food and drink stalls, a Riverside Pavilion and also a lovely courtyard café and restaurant at the entrance. Indoors there is a restaurant with hot food and traditional lunch choices. As a visit to the castle can be quite lengthy, it is worth factoring in a meal or refreshments to help bolster energy levels and rest the legs mid-exploration.

◆ *Head to Warwick's green spaces for traditional picnic fun*

Entertainment

The town comes alive on weekends when the pubs and bars, particularly in warmer weather, spill out on to the streets. Cocktail lounges and restaurants attract an older local crowd, from aged 25 upwards. It is not a town known for its clubbing scene; you are better off catching a bus, train or cab the short distance to Leamington Spa if you are in search of nightclubs, but some of the bars have late licences.

The numerous traditional pubs are always busy with revellers, and many have a historic significance, like the Millwright Arms, which dates from around 1600, and at one time was used as a poorhouse, providing accommodation for the most needy. Visitors will delight in the fact that nearly all Warwick's pubs have a long history as drinking establishments, and as such are usually full of character – and indeed characters.

For live music the larger acts can be seen at the **Assembly** in Leamington Spa (see page 83); however, some pubs, restaurants and wine bars play host to smaller, local bands. Classical or traditional music evenings are often held at the **Lord Leycester Hospital** (see page 67) and the **Collegiate Church of St Mary** (see page 54).

The University of Warwick, which rather confusingly is closer to Coventry, is also home to the **Warwick Arts Centre**, but it's well worth making a trip here, as the programme of theatre, comedy and performing arts is excellent. Theatre is also available in town, particularly for young people at the **Playbox Theatre** in the specially designed **Dream Factory** (ⓦ www.playboxtheatre.com) and also at Warwick School, where

the **Bridge House Theatre** (Ⓦ www.bridgehousetheatre.co.uk)
is used by visiting performers and the local community
alike. Tickets for both can be found online or booked directly at
the sites.

As with all elements of Warwick life, the castle also plays a
central role in entertaining locals and tourists, with a year-round
programme of events, including re-enactments, dungeon visits
and banquets.

⬥ Drink in a splash of culture at Warwick Arts Centre

Sport & relaxation

For a small town, Warwick actually has a long tradition of sporting participation and success. It also offers a range of activities and spectator sports for the visitor.

ADVENTURE

As a town surrounded by countryside, there are opportunities for many activities. **Adventure Sports**, off the A425 (ⓐ Wedgnock Lane ⓣ 01926 491948 ⓦ www.adventuresport.co.uk ⓛ Dependent on booking) offers quad biking, clay-pigeon shooting, 4WD off-roading and much more.

CRICKET
Warwickshire County Cricket
As a county, Warwickshire has a long and illustrious history in cricket, with the first-known county team playing near the racecourse in 1826. By 1886 they had moved to Edgbaston.

The main entrance to Edgbaston is on Pershore Road (A441). By car from Warwick head north on the M40, join the M42, leaving at Junction 3. Follow the A435 towards Birmingham. ⓐ Edgbaston Rd, Birmingham ⓣ 0870 062 1902 ⓦ www.edgbaston.com ⓛ The season runs from April to September. Tickets are on sale from April ⓝ Bus: 45, 47; Train: Birmingham New Street, Birmingham Snow Hill

The local team, **Warwick Cricket Club** (ⓐ Hampton Road ⓣ 01926 491569 ⓦ www.warwickcricketclub.com ⓔ warwickcricketclub@hotmail.com) play in the Warwickshire Cricket League.

GOLF

Warwick Golf Centre is a nine-hole course that is based at the racecourse; ring beforehand for times as there is no golfing on race days or before 12.30. ⓐ Hampton Street ⓣ 01926 494316

HORSE RACING

Warwick Racecourse

Hosting races since 1707, this is one of the oldest grounds in the country. There are both flat and jump race meetings all year round. Adult ticket prices are £15.00 Monday to Friday, £18.00 on weekends. Discounts and other offers are available online.

The entrance is on Hampton Street, a ten-minute walk from the town centre. If driving leave the M40 and follow the A429. Warwick train station is 1.2 km (¾ mile) away. ⓐ Hampton Street ⓣ 08445 793013 ⓦ www.warwickracecourse.co.uk ⓛ Race times vary, from midday onwards ⓝ Train: Warwick Station 1.2 km (¾ mile) from the racecourse

🔺 *Tee off at the racecourse-based golf centre*

Accommodation

Warwick and the surrounding areas have a good variety of accommodation, from quaint little B&Bs to large, comfortable hotels and farm stays. Visitors will delight in the attractive town-centre accommodation, which tends to be in historic Tudor or Georgian buildings, with many conveniently located near the sights. Being deep in the heart of some of England's most picturesque countryside, there are also some great camping options.

GUESTHOUSES

Avon Guest House £ A lovely old building, the Avon dates back to 1840 and retains many fine features, including some original flagstone flooring. Opposite St Nicholas Park, the guesthouse feels more like a family home. Rooms have DVD players, fridges and wireless Internet access and there's a choice between eight rooms in the main house and two in a separate converted coach house. ⊙ 7 Emscote Road ❶ 01926 491367 ⓦ www.avonguesthouse.gbr.cc ⊖ info@avonguesthouse.co.uk

Charter House £ If it's atmosphere you're after, then Charter House's award-winning medieval theme is bound to fit the bill. A 15th-century Grade II listed building, it has three large rooms, one overlooking an old English garden in the castle ground. The owner is famous for her hospitality and great breakfasts. All rooms have their own facilities. ⊙ 87–91 West Street ❶ 01926 496965 ❶ 01296 411910

Seven Stars £ With only three rooms, this charmingly traditional Grade II listed building is worth booking. Great value, oak-beamed rooms, quaintly accommodated bathrooms (tiny doors but decent size), off-street parking and an excellent location near the racecourse add to friendly hosts and a good breakfast.
ⓐ 50 Friars Street ⓣ 01926 492658
ⓦ www.sevenstarswarwick.co.uk
ⓔ info@sevenstarswarwick.co.uk

Park Cottage ££ Stay in your own piece of castle property at Park Cottage, located at the entrance to Warwick Castle, a 15th-century, Grade II listed, timber-framed property initially belonging to the Earl of Warwick. Once within the castle boundaries, the breakfast room used to be the castle dairy. It has seven uniquely styled rooms, a private car park and a garden that boasts a 300-year-old yew tree. Homely touches make it that extra-bit special. ⓐ 113 West Street ⓣ 01926 410319
ⓦ www.parkcottagewarwick.co.uk
ⓔ janet@parkcottagewarwick.co.uk

HOTELS

The Lord Leycester Hotel ££ Just a two-minute walk from the castle, all 48 rooms in this large Georgian three-star hotel are en-suite and the Stratford Bar and Jesters Brasserie are on hand for drinks and refreshments. At the heart of hotel is a stone building, originally called Jury Street House, dating from the late 16th century, which has been extended to include neighbouring buildings. Opening as a hotel in 1926, it had Henry Ford as an early guest. The car park accommodates up to 40 cars. Try to

book the four-poster room for that something extra.
ⓐ Jury Street ⓣ 01926 491481 ⓦ www.lord-leycester.co.uk
ⓔ reception@lord-leycester.co.uk

Warwick Arms Hotel ££ For a hotel atmosphere in the centre of town, the charming Warwick Arms is a great option. Another building owned by the earls of Warwick, this is the oldest established hotel in the area, with a history that can be traced back to 1591, although the original building burnt down in the great fire of 1694. The current building was built in 1717, with neighbouring properties subsequently taken over. Behind the traditional façade lies a modern, boutique-style 40-roomed hotel. Its lovely bar and lounge are ideal for a break during the day for guests and visitors alike. ⓐ High Street ⓣ 01926 492759 ⓦ www.warwickarmshotel.com
ⓔ reception@warwickarmshotel.com

RURAL FARM STAYS

If you have a car and want to stay somewhere out of town there are several great options.

Hill Farm and Shepherd's Hut £ A 16-km (10-mile) drive from Warwick, this 450-acre working farm has three farmhouse rooms and an original 1800s shepherd's hut to stay in. Horses, a flock of breeding ewes, a small herd of cows and corn are all housed on site. There are far-reaching views and wonderful walks to be taken through the fields. For real rural romance the wood-lined shepherd's hut is open from Easter until the end of September. It has its own private area with outdoor seats and a barbecue, a double bed and heating. ⓐ Priors Hardwick, near Southam ⓣ 01327 260338 ⓦ www.stayathillfarm.co.uk

Redlands Farm £ Set in an acre of Warwickshire countryside, 10 km (6 miles) from Warwick, the farm dates from the early 1600s, the time of Charles I, and boasts its own 'priest hole', built to hide priests from persecution. Now lovingly restored, the three oak-beamed rooms are en-suite and there is access to a small kitchen if needed. The best thing is the proximity to the countryside – there are marvellous views overlooking an orchard, and chickens provide fresh eggs for breakfast. There's also an outdoor swimming pool and barbecue area. ⓐ Banbury Rd, Lighthorne ⓣ 01926 651241

CAMPING

The proximity of the green belt makes for some great camping options further afield. For something different, **Warwick Racecourse** also has an adjacent Caravan Club-approved campsite for camping vehicles only (no tents), the novelty of which is you have to cross the racecourse to get there. Room is restricted on race days, but it's a pretty site and ideally placed for Warwick's attractions. ⓐ Hampton Street ⓣ 01926 495448 ⓦ www.warwickracecourse.co.uk

THE BEST OF WARWICK

Whether it's history, culture or the more modern-day
pursuits of shopping, eating out or sipping cocktails after
dark, Warwick has a healthy supply of all.

TOP 10 ATTRACTIONS

- **Warwick Castle** Tread the flagstones of thousands of
  years of history in one of the world's best-preserved
  medieval castles, with a bit of Disney-esque magic thrown
  in (see page 42).

- **Mill Street & Mill Garden** Breathtaking gardens with an
  unbeatable castle and river backdrop. Expect a stunning
  view around every herbaceous corner (see pages 49 & 47).

- **Collegiate Church of St Mary** Magnificent early 12th-
  century church, visible for miles. A beautiful interior, a
  spooky crypt and a 134-step climb for unparalleled views
  (see page 54).

- **The Lord Leycester Hospital & Master's Garden** Fine-
  looking timbered 14th- and 15th-century home to
  medieval guilds, with the delightful Master's Garden and
  The Queen's Own Hussars Museum (see page 67).

- **St John's House Museum** Striking Jacobean mansion incorporating an interesting collection and The Royal Regiment of Fusiliers (Royal Warwickshire) museum (see page 57).

- **Shopping on Smith Street** Medieval shopping street, survivor of the great fire of 1694 and current home to quirky shops and atmospheric eateries (see page 57).

- **A day at the races** Have a flutter or simply soak in the charged atmosphere at one of England's oldest racecourses (see page 69).

- **Saltisford Canal Centre** A green and watery oasis restored in the once derelict Saltisford Arm of the Grand Union Canal. Refreshments and boat hire in a converted canal warehouse (see page 58).

- **Go to market** The very foundation of Warwick, apart from the castle, the weekly, modern-day incarnation of the old market (see page 73).

- **Time for tea** Whether it's just for a cuppa, a light lunch or a full-blown afternoon tea, Warwick's several historic tea rooms can indulge every fancy.

⯆ *Extravagant tombs in the opulent interior of St Mary's Church*

Suggested itineraries

HALF-DAY: WARWICK IN A HURRY

Many visitors just head to Warwick for the castle, which is a shame, as this characterful small town has a lot more to offer besides. That said, if you really can only spend a short time in Warwick, then you do have to visit this historical wonder. With half a day at your disposal, make sure you spend at least two hours in the castle and cover the bare essentials (the Kingmaker exhibition and grounds tour would give you a good overview) before heading to lunch at one of the eateries in the centre of town, then enjoying the shops on Jury Street, Swan Street and Smith Street.

1 DAY: TIME TO SEE A LITTLE MORE

Start with breakfast in one of the cafés around Market Place to stand you in good stead for some serious castle action. Three to four hours should cover the main exhibits and a pre-allotted slot for the superb Castle Dungeon. Don't miss the Kingmaker exhibition, State Rooms and A Royal Weekend Party. If you time it well, you might also catch a bird-of-prey show or some jousting. Stop for tea in the Undercroft or, weather permitting, buy something tasty from one of the stalls within the grounds.

Before lunch, nip behind the castle to see Mill Garden, then stroll into town for a late lunch. Spend the rest of the day browsing antique shops and boutiques around town. As evening falls, take advantage of the range of traditional pubs and enjoy a pint or two in historic surroundings. With an appetite worked up, it's time for an evening meal at one of Warwick's restaurants.

2–3 DAYS: SHORT CITY BREAK

With more time at your disposal, you can see the castle as above but take more time to explore the gardens and perhaps spend one evening there enjoying a banquet. Add a day at the racecourse and take your pick of Warwick's excellent museums. If you fancy some fresh-air fun, enjoy a break in the parks or a canal boat trip; and if you're there on Saturday, make sure you visit the market.

LONGER: ENJOYING WARWICK TO THE FULL

Once the delights of Warwick have been fully explored, head to nearby **Leamington Spa** (see page 80) for fantastic shopping and a livelier nightlife. Go further afield to the Cotswolds for picture-perfect villages and take a trip to Shakespeare's town of **Stratford-upon-Avon** (see page 84) to enjoy further fascinating sights.

⬤ Take a jaunt to Stratford-upon-Avon and visit Shakespeare's birthplace

Something for nothing

The wealth of medieval architecture means a walk through Warwick is a free cultural activity in itself. Start near the train station and browse the buildings at Coten End before making your way past St Nicholas Church towards Mill Street for some of the finest timbered houses in town. Retrace your steps up to Smith Street and window-shop your way up to Eastgate, then walk along Jury Street and High Street towards Westgate by The Lord Leycester Hospital. Many of the museums are free to visit, including the imposing St John's House, perfect for children with its toys, dolls and games collection. Admission is also free to The Warwickshire County Museum in Market Hall (see page 69) and its fascinating natural history exhibits.

WARWICK'S GREEN SPACES

Warwick is ringed by green spaces and, since the 1930s, St Nicholas Park has played a central role in local outdoor life. It's perfect for picnics, games and walks along the river. Children's facilities include a play area, paddling pool, roundabouts, adventure golf and giant chess. There are also football pitches and tennis courts and there's ample space for ball games.

In town you'll find Pageant Field, a lawned retreat, and Priory Park, known for its magnificent trees. Tucked behind the Collegiate Church of St Mary, down the quaintly named Tink a Tank Lane, is a small but delightful walled garden.

When it rains

There are many rainy-day options to keep visitors of all ages entertained in the great indoors in Warwick, not least of all at the castle, where all major exhibitions and main rooms are located inside. There is nothing more atmospheric than wandering the State Rooms, with rain pattering on the castle windows, and wondering how on earth they managed to keep the huge stone rooms warm in winters gone by. The dark and dingy depths of the Castle Dungeon also take on a new level of suitable gloom when it is grey and wet outside.

A rainy day is also an ideal opportunity to take your time exploring the museums and galleries. Medieval houses are perfect for cosy days indoors, and The Lord Leycester Hospital's charming rooms are well worth exploring on a wet day.

To keep restless children occupied, head to the toys and games of St John's House Museum, where there are lots of activities to amuse. They can find out what it was like to be a child in the Victorian era. Children under 12 can be amused at Funky Monkey's in Cattell Road, which has a large 'jungle' play area and a whole host of soft and safe indoor 'rough and tumble' games, as well as a juice bar and café for parents.

Warwick's wood-panelled, historic pubs are also tempting when it's cold or wet outside, and many are equipped with large TV screens on which you can catch the day's sports. Do also make time to browse the bookshops, especially the excellent Warwick Books, a family-run library-like shop. If your visit coincides with the October book festival, Warwick Words, you are in for a treat.

On arrival

Warwick is located very much in the centre of rural England, so it's easy to get to from most directions, with the nearest big cities being Birmingham to the north and Coventry to the east.

ARRIVING BY CAR

The M40 is the easiest and most major route to Warwick and it runs from London all the way to Birmingham. The M1 runs from London to Leeds; take the exit towards Coventry and Rugby.

From the south, head north from London on the M40, exiting at junction 13. Turn right on to the A452 and then at the roundabout take the second exit on to the A425 and follow this into Warwick.

From the north (Birmingham), follow the A34 until you reach the M42. Take the left branch of the road at junction 3a, which will allow you to join the M40. Stay on the M40 until junction 15 then, at the Longbridge roundabout, take the second exit on to the A429 and straight into Warwick.

Parking

There are 14 council car parks in town, all pay and display. Charges for these vary, but usually are between 70p and 90p an hour, around £1.50 for two hours and up to a maximum of £8. Car parks are situated in Castle Lane, Westgate, The Butts, Priory Road, Barrack Street, Linen Street and St Nicholas Park, and are clearly signposted. There is also parking at the racecourse and at Warwick Castle.

There is no charge for drivers displaying a disabled badge in any of the council-run car parks. Disabled drivers are also entitled to unlimited parking on single yellow lines (providing you do not cause an obstruction) and two hours' free parking on double yellow lines.

ARRIVING BY AIR

Birmingham International Airport operates flights to and from many UK and European destinations and to some destinations further afield. It is just over 27 km (17 miles) and a 30-minute drive from the airport to Warwick. Follow the A452 and then the A4177.

Taxis from the airport to Warwick are readily available.

◆ Centrally located Warwick is easily reached by car, plane and train

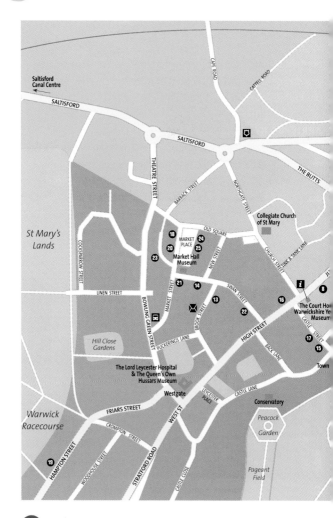

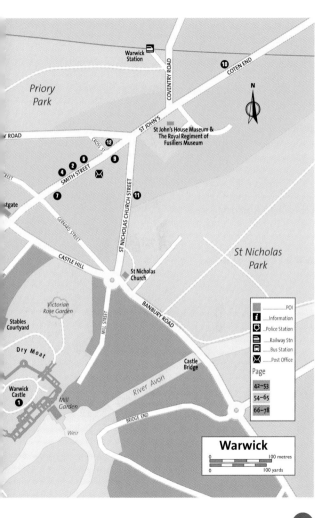

ARRIVING BY TRAIN

From Warwick train station it is just a short walk to the castle and the centre of town. There are frequent, fast and direct services to and from London and Birmingham Snow Hill.

If taking the train from the airport at Birmingham International, there are two options – to change at Birmingham Snow Hill for the direct service to Warwick, or change at Leamington Spa for another direct service to Warwick. Total journey time should take about 50 minutes, including the change.

Warwick Parkway station is slightly further out than Warwick main station, about 2.5 km (1½ miles) to the west of town, but most services run through both stations.

ARRIVING BY COACH

Warwick's main bus station is found on Bowling Green Street, and coaches from London, Birmingham, Birmingham International, East Midlands Airport, Oxford, Coventry and other key UK cities all stop here.

FINDING YOUR FEET

Dominated as it is by the castle walls and the steeple of the Collegiate Church of St Mary, it is very difficult to lose your bearings in this small town. An hour's stroll around Warwick should give you a good overview of the centre, as well as revealing the key sites and attractions. Overall it is a very safe town, with low crime rates and a generally affluent, upwardly mobile population. As with all areas popular with tourists, it can get very busy, particularly on weekends or at peak holiday times; however there are no significant dangers or annoyances. Take as much care as you would at home when walking around after dark.

ORIENTATION

Starting in the northeast of Warwick, as you would arrive if coming from Leamington Spa or if walking into town from the main train station, Coten End, leading on to St John's, takes you right into town, with one of the key sights, St John's House Museum, immediately visible on your left. The road forks into three, so either head straight down Smith Street for the shops and medieval architecture, or south along St Nicholas Church Street for Mill Street and the back of Warwick Castle. From there a short walk up Castle Hill to the left brings you to the heart of Warwick town. Although most of the town is accessible to cars, it is also very pedestrian friendly and virtually impossible to get lost. Market Place, the castle or the tower of St Mary's are always close at hand to help you navigate your way.

GETTING AROUND

Warwick is a small town and there's no need to use public transport unless you want to head further out to Leamington Spa or take a trip to the Cotswolds. Local taxi firms are available if your accommodation is on the outskirts of town, but for sightseeing around Warwick itself you really are better off donning some comfy shoes and hitting the pavement. There are plenty of nice green spots and cafés to rest the legs every now and then. The main part of town is also flat and easy to negotiate for wheelchairs or pushchairs. Pavements are not particularly wide but the traffic is tourist-aware. It can get very busy on weekends and holidays, so expect to stroll rather than walk with purpose.

Buses out of town

All buses leave from Warwick bus station on Bowling Green Street, which is centrally located just off Market Street. The X18 goes to Leamington Spa; the X17 goes to Warwick Hospital, Warwick rail station, Leamington Spa, Kenilworth and Coventry; the number 16 goes to Stratford-upon-Avon.

CAR HIRE

Cars can be hired easily and relatively inexpensively in Warwick, particularly if booked in advance. A car is not necessary if you are just planning to visit Warwick centre, but if you want to explore the surrounding countryside, car hire is recommended. There is a mix of local and nationally known names available, with cars from as little as £29 a day to classic vehicles at a great deal more.

Enterprise Rent-A-Car ⓐ Leamington Spa Railway Station, Old Warwick Road, Leamington Spa ⓣ 01926 885866

Newtown Vehicle Rentals Ltd ⓐ 73 Emscote Road, Warwick ⓣ 01926 499831

Xtra Wheels ⓐ Unit 4 Benford Court, Lower Cape, Warwick ⓣ 01926 490687

For something extra special, **The Open Road** have a selection of vintage classic and sports cars. ⓐ Market Square, Warwick ⓣ 0845 070 5142

▶ *The Lord Leycester Hospital, a superb timber building*

THE CITY OF
Warwick

Introduction to city areas

For the purposes of the guide, the town has been divided into three sections. The first, **Warwick Castle and around** covers the castle and its extensive grounds, with over 60 acres of buildings and gardens, which in total consume almost a third of Warwick's footprint. Immediately outside the castle boundaries, the surrounding roads retain almost a countryside feel, with quiet rows of cottages on Castle Lane, cleverly concealed parking and Mill Street's timbered houses and famous garden.

The second section focuses on the area **North of the castle**. Reaching out from the middle of the castle at Town Gate, from Castle Street to Church Street to Northgate Street, up to Priory Park at the north and east to Coten End, the northern part of town is home to the Collegiate Church of St Mary, Jury Street and Smith Street, as well as the green spaces of St Nicholas Park and Priory Park and the timbered houses that stretch northeast towards Leamington Spa.

The third section, **West of the castle**, looks at the area that spreads out from the castle to the west, taking in everything south of Church Street and Shire Hall, including Market Place, and the shops, bars and restaurants on High Street and Jury Street, across to the racecourse and St Mary's Lands.

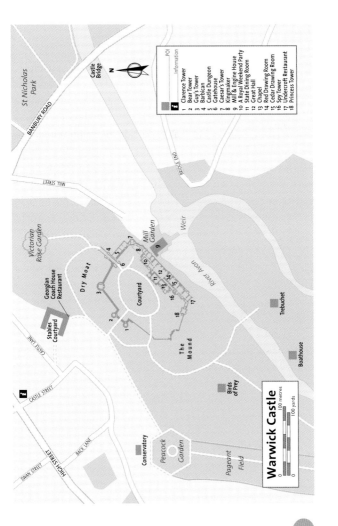

Warwick Castle

POI
— — Information

1 Clarence Tower
2 Bear Tower
3 Guy's Tower
4 Barbican
5 Castle Dungeon
6 Gatehouse
7 Caesar's Tower
8 Kingmaker
9 Mill & Engine House
10 A Royal Weekend Party
11 State Dining Room
12 Great Hall
13 Chapel
14 Red Drawing Room
15 Cedar Drawing Room
16 Spy Tower
17 Undercroft Restaurant
18 Princess Tower

Warwick Castle & around

The main draw for many a Warwick visitor, **Warwick Castle**, a stunning feat of medieval construction, deserves its reputation as one of the finest preserved medieval castles in the UK. With a history spanning over 1,100 years (see box page 46), the castle is still a focal point of town life, now as a major tourist attraction rather than a fortification at the centre of centuries of battles. The juxtaposition of modern-day entertainment and history is what transforms Warwick Castle from monument to great day out for people of all ages. Die-hard historians might not approve of the Disney-fication of the castle, but it is now firmly on the tourist map as a must-see attraction, which should help keep the castle alive for future generations. As well as the attractions listed below, the castle hosts frequent activities such as jousting, bird-of-prey flying and summer musical concerts (see page 50) as well as themed evening banquets (see box page 52).

Entrance to the castle is via a picturesque courtyard at Castle Lane, where there is also a car park; the main car park is to the southwest of the castle on Stratford Road. The castle covers a large area, and there are a lot of stairs in some parts, so do wear comfortable shoes. There are some accessibility limitations. You will need to allow a good 4–5 hours for your visit to be able to properly appreciate the castle and grounds. ⓐ Castle Hill ❶ 0870 442 2000 ⓦ www.warwick-castle.co.uk ❺ 10.00–18.00 daily (Apr–Sept); 10.00–17.00 daily (Oct–Mar), closed Christmas Day ❶ Admission charge; last entry half an hour before closing

SIGHTS & ATTRACTIONS

Castle Dungeon

It is 1345 and Warwick is gripped by the deadly plague. Live characters bring to life (and death) the dark, decaying stench of doom, the torturers' horrific methods and implements, such as the hook and the tongue-tearer, and there are chanting monks and a mirrored maze.

The dungeons as an exhibit were only added in 2009 and, run by the same firm that runs the London Dungeon and Madame Tussauds, are now more theatre than anything. But adults and older children alike will love the darkly comic

◆ *Beautiful Mill Garden overlooks the castle*

performances of the doctor, the executioner and the wholly
biased judge. Audience participation is often asked for, so if you
don't want to get too close to the action, stand towards the
back of the group. The experience is designed to be scarily
authentic, so children under the age of 15 have to be
accompanied by an adult and it may not be suitable for those
aged under 10. You have been warned!

The grounds

First used as a vantage point for military protection, **The Mound**
formed one of the earliest defences at Warwick. In the early
1600s, Sir Fulke Greville started the planting of the extensive
gardens, helping transform the castle from a fortress to an
opulent private home. From the 17th century onwards,
The Mound was mere decoration and today provides stunning
views of the grounds and beyond.

One of the most celebrated of landscape architects of all
time, Lancelot 'Capability' Brown started work on the grounds in
1749. Sweeping upwards from the moat, the gardens still retain
Brown's signature undulating lawns and winding paths,
something that was quite a departure from the traditionally
more formal arrangements of the time.

The eye-catching **Conservatory**, built in 1786, was originally
designed to show off the Warwick Vase, a beautiful example of
Roman pottery found near Tivoli in 1771. Now replaced by a
replica, the original is on display at the Burrell Collection in
Glasgow and the Conservatory is used as a glasshouse, as it was
in Victorian times. Standing at the Conservatory and looking
towards the river is one of the best views in town.

The **Peacock Garden**, at the front of the Conservatory, was designed by Victorian landscape gardener Robert Marnock; leading down to the river, the **Pageant Field** has some stunning examples of 200-year-old trees, one of which was planted by Prince Albert in 1858.

On the island in centre of the river stands the largest working trebuchet in the world, weighing a hefty 22 tonnes and standing 18 m (59 ft) high. Catch one of the regular demonstrations of its awesome power.

▲ *A vista of the castle's impressive grounds*

THE CASTLE HISTORY

Two years after his 1066 victory at Hastings, William the Conqueror established a motte-and-bailey fort on The Mound above the Avon. By 1220 most of the original wooden structure had been replaced by stone, with a wall over 7 m (23 ft) high encasing a chapel, great hall, two imposing towers and a gate. By the 14th century the castle had become a towering medieval fortress, frequently attacked, besieged and changing hands until, as a reflection of altering times, it gradually morphed from a strategic military stronghold to a lavish and opulent residence.

The Civil War saw the castle besieged once more in 1642, though unsuccessfully, and the castle, now occupied by the Greville family, oversaw fortification of its defences. Cannons and gun emplacements were added, as was the Gaol, where Royalist prisoners were held.

By the 17th century, in an England more peaceful than at any time in living memory, the living quarters, new dining room and other extensions were developed, adding a lavish elegance more suited to the burgeoning upper classes. Landscaper 'Capability' Brown oversaw a redesign to the outside spaces, now given more to entertaining and impressing rather than warring and defence. The balls and parties continued until the 1970s, when the castle was sold to a private company and development into the attraction it is today began.

The **Victorian Rose Garden** was also created by Robert Marnock, in 1868. Having rather uncaringly been smothered by a tennis court sometime in the early part of the 20th century, the design was brought back to life in the 1980s and follows original drawings. When the flowers are in full bloom (June and July) it is very easy to appreciate the Victorians' admiration for the old-fashioned rose.

Kingmaker

Another interactive exhibit takes visitors to deep within the walls, in one of the oldest parts of the castle, where the date is 1471 and the Kingmaker, Richard Neville, Earl of Warwick, is preparing for the Battle of Barnet during the long War of the Roses. Blacksmiths are crafting armour, weapons are being made and sharpened and food is being cooked to take to battle. The sights, sounds and smells create an atmospheric and educational exhibit.

Mill & Engine House

The Mill and Engine House have been on their current site at the foot of the castle walls since the 14th century, but in the 1880s a fire destroyed everything except the waterwheel and the outer walls. Electrical equipment was installed in 1894, making the castle one of the first private residences in England to have electric lights. After a £2 million restoration project, the Mill tells a fascinating tale of Victorian industrial triumph.

Mill Garden

A veritable oasis at the foot of the castle, the Mill Garden was originally created by Arthur Measures, who tended the garden

● *Position, focus, release (and hope)!*

for over 60 years, and it was once part of the castle grounds. Now in the hands of his daughter, Julia, it's open to the public from April to October. The trees, flowers, shrubs and winding paths are a pleasure to meander. Painterly views of the Mill, medieval bridge remains and the river are abundant as the cottage garden changes through the seasons. ⓐ 55 Mill Street ● 09.00–18.00 daily (1 Apr–31 Oct) ① Adult admission charge, accompanying children free

Mill Street

Behind the castle walls, leading down to the riverside, Mill
Street is one of the most picturesque medieval streets in
England, with rows of Tudor houses that contrived to survive the
great fire of 1694. Although this was once the main entrance
into the castle and the mill to which it owes its name, and
therefore quite a busy thoroughfare, the cobbled street now
only leads down to the Mill Garden (see above). The medieval
bridge that spanned the river near the garden fell down in the
18th century, but parts of this can still be seen. Expansion of the
castle has split the Mill from Mill Street and the Mill Garden.
ⓐ Mill Street, behind the castle

A Royal Weekend Party

The peak of the castle's party days were presided over by Daisy,
Countess of Warwick in the 1890s, and this wonderful exhibit
welcomes you as a guest to one of these auspicious occasions.
The atmosphere is one of anticipation as the guests (including
Edward Prince of Wales, a young Winston Churchill and a
plethora of dukes and duchesses) prepare for what promises to
be a wildly indulgent weekend in this sumptuously decorated
part of the castle.

State Rooms

With each castle resident wanting to make their mark, the
medieval State Rooms, with bare beginnings in the 14th century,
have been extended and embellished to create an opulent place
to live and entertain. They include a 1600s chapel, the lovely
lacquered Red Drawing Room, the lavish State Dining Room,

commissioned in 1763, the magnificent Cedar Drawing Room and the largest and most important room in the castle, the Great Hall.

Towers and ramparts

For far-reaching views of the castle and beyond, make the climb to Guy's Tower and Caesar's Tower, along the walkways where crossbowmen and archers once protected the fortress. The Princess Tower (for younger children – adults only allowed at arranged times) is now home to Arabella, a 'fairytale princess', who is getting reading for a castle wedding in a pink-decorated, magical boudoir. The Gaol, the lowest chamber of Caesar's Tower, brings you back down to earth, with its walls bearing inscriptions carved by Royalist prisoners in the English Civil War.

CULTURE

Warwick Castle concerts

The superb setting is ideal for outdoor music concerts, held during the summer, and also forms the dramatic backdrop to the popular annual 'Carols at the Castle'. Summer concert-goers can bring along a picnic and enjoy a feast while listening to the music, as well as relishing the spectacular fireworks display at evening's end. There is a varied programme of events, including a Summer Proms with headline British acts. See website or phone for details. ⓐ Castle Hill ⓣ 0870 442 2000 ⓦ www.warwick-castle.co.uk

RETAIL THERAPY

While the castle and surrounding areas are not exactly a haven for shopping, fear not, because the rest of Warwick more than makes up for it. There are two traditional **gift shops** in the castle selling mugs, pens, postcards, those 'essential' prosthetic dungeon masks, plastic swords, sweets, fudges, old maps and all things Warwick.

Outside the castle, the **Thomas Oken Tea Rooms** (see page 74) has a quaint little shop area selling English rose crockery, a range of jams and chutneys, real ales, pictures of Old Warwick and an impressive 22 different types of loose-leaf tea.

⬤ *Flags fly high at Warwick Castle*

CAROUSING AT THE CASTLE

Pre-booking is essential for most themed evenings at the castle (see page 42 for contact details).

Dungeons After Dark

For all who dare, this is an evening of entertainment, food and wine. A seasonal meal is served and guests are encouraged to dress to impress the ghosts and ghouls.

Kingmakers Mediaeval Banquet

The vaulted 14th-century Undercroft Restaurant is the location for this four-course meal with changing themes.

Highwayman's Supper

A secret tour of the State Rooms is followed by a banquet in the Coach House, which 'risks' an encounter with the dastardly highwayman himself.

TAKING A BREAK

Castle refreshments £–££ ❶ Within the castle walls there are many options for refreshments and indeed you might find a break is welcome, as there is a lot of walking and sightseeing to be done. The **Georgian Coach House Restaurant** – within Stables Courtyard at the entrance to the castle – serves breakfasts, lunches and a selection of scones, cakes and puddings until 16.00. The **Undercroft Restaurant**, off the

Haunted Castle After Dark tours

These evening events run in the last week of October and, although light-hearted and festive, have a fair dose of scary activity – so those of a nervous disposition are warned against them, as are children under 10.

Christmas

The Mediaeval Banquet takes on a Christmas theme and is supplemented by Candlelit Tours, an atmospheric way to visit the castle. Characters from Christmas past visit and you can enjoy mulled wine and mince pies.

New Year's Eve

For something really special, spend New Year's Eve at the castle, at the Great Hall Mediaeval Banquet. Guests enjoy a five-course meal, entertainment, and then a glass of champagne and a ceilidh as they welcome in the New Year.

central courtyard, is within the lower level of the castle and is an atmospherically vaulted room serving traditional British roasts, hot and cold meals and puddings. Cream teas are a speciality.

Depending on the time of year, you will also find seasonal food stalls within the castle grounds, serving everything from waffles to ice cream to fish and chips, as well as a coffee cart for hot drinks. In warmer months the lawns are always very popular for picnics, especially next to the Riverside Pavilion.

North of the castle

The area reaching out from the centre of the castle, up to Priory Park and along to Coten End, holds some of the finest examples of those Tudor houses that survived the great fire, as well as some Georgian masterpieces. It is easy to negotiate on foot and a stroll from Castle Street to the end of Smith Street could only take a few minutes, depending on how many shops you are distracted by.

SIGHTS & ATTRACTIONS

Collegiate Church of St Mary (St Mary's Church)

The tower of St Mary's is as much a part of the Warwick landscape as the castle. One of the largest and most important churches in England, it's also a much-heralded piece of Gothic architecture. As well as being a full working church with a regular congregation, inside is a veritable who's who of tombs for Warwick's key figures over the centuries. There are four choirs based at St Mary's, a tradition that goes back over a thousand years, and frequent choral and musical gatherings are listed in the church calendar.

Parts of the church date back to 1123 when it was founded by the second Earl of Warwick. The great fire of 1694 destroyed the original tower, but it was rebuilt ten years later by local architect brothers, Francis and William Smith. The crypt is part of the original Norman building and showcases a rarely preserved part of a medieval ducking stool. This grim relic of the Middle Ages was used as a punishment for women who had been accused of witchcraft, prostitution, or even of being 'scolds' or gossips; they were strapped into the chair and ducked into freezing water. ⓐ Old Square ⓣ 01926 400771 ⓦ www.stmaryswarwick.org.uk ⓛ 10.00–18.00 daily (Apr–Oct); 10.00–16.30 daily (Nov–Mar) ⓘ Admission to the tower is charged; there is also a suggested donation to the church of £2

The Court House

Designed by Francis Smith, of St Mary's Church fame, the imposing Court House, completed in 1731, is a fine example of the type of Georgian building that replaced the gaps left by the

◖ The building of St John's House Museum is a treat in itself

Great Fire some 30 years previously. The Court House is now home to the **Tourist Information Centre** and also houses the **Warwickshire Yeomanry Museum**. Military enthusiasts will enjoy the collection of uniforms, weapons, medals and memorabilia. ⓐ Jury Street ① 01926 492212 ⓦ www.visitwarwick.co.uk ⓒ 09.00–16.30 Mon–Fri, 10.00–16.30 Sat, 10.00–15.30 Sun

Eastgate

One of three remaining gates into William the Conqueror's early Warwick, Eastgate was reconstructed in the 15th century and remodelled in 1788. The building was used as a school classroom for several years but in 2010 was sold to a local couple who plan to let the building for holiday accommodation. ⓐ Corner of Smith Street and Castle Hill

🔺 *Step back in time at St John's House Museum*

St John's House

This imposing example of 17th-century Jacobean architecture has a peaceful garden and is home to two fascinating museums (see below). ⓐ St John's, Warwick ⓣ 01926 412 021 ⓦ www.warwickshire.gov.uk/museum

Smith Street

Leading down from Eastgate is another of Warwick's best examples of medieval timbered housing. Landor House, built in 1692 and one-time home of the poet Walter Savage Landor, stands out at the top of the street; opposite this are several more excellent examples of fine Tudor buildings. At numbers 27 and 28, further down the hill, some Venetian windows are still intact. ⓦ www.warwick-smithstreet.co.uk

CULTURE

St John's House Museum

Inside St John's House is an extensive and fascinating social history collection. The exhibitions are very child-friendly, showing how Victorian children lived, with plenty of opportunities to interact. A costume and textile collection shows clothing worn by local people over the last 200 years. 'Object Corner' includes a large cardboard wedding cake used by brides and grooms in the Second World War, for whom rationing put an end to the edible variety, and the collection even includes a mobile phone from the year 2000 which, to some, now justifiably belongs in a museum.

St John's House also houses **The Royal Regiment of Fusiliers (Royal Warwickshire) Museum** (ⓣ 01926 491653

ⓦ www.warwickfusiliers.co.uk). Visitors are welcomed by a soldier from the year 1744; the museum tells the tale of the 6th Foot division of the Royal Warwickshire Regiment via weapons, uniforms, pictures and other objects. ⓐ St John's House ⓣ 01926 412021 ⓦ www.warwickshire.gov.uk/museum ⓛ 10.00–17.00 Tues, Sat & bank holidays, 14.30–17.00 Sun (Apr–Sept only)

Saltisford Canal Centre

The Saltisford Arm was the terminus of the Warwick and Birmingham Canal, first developed in the 1790s. This was a key Industrial Revolution trade route, helping to link London, Liverpool, Bristol and Hull. However, by the 1970s, with large-scale canal transport almost obsolete, the Saltisford Arm was abandoned.

Renovated by the Saltisford Canal Trust, it's now home to several families living afloat, many of whom have created their own gardens, and managed by the charity. It's a peaceful place to visit, amid orchards, gardens and the waterway, and a favourite for visiting narrow boats. There are picnic tables, a barbecue area and a small shop with refreshments in a converted canalside warehouse. Day boat hire is also available. ⓐ Budbrooke Road ⓣ 01926 490006 ⓦ www.saltisfordcanal. co.uk ⓛ 09.30–17.30 daily ⓘ Not all facilities are available every day ⓝ Bus: 66

RETAIL THERAPY

Just as it must have delighted shoppers down the centuries, Smith Street still charms the 21st-century shopper with its independent boutiques, bookshops and quirky retailers.

◓ *Enjoy a day messing about on the canal*

Be Gorgeous Owner Lindsey Roberts buys all the clothes for her independent boutique, aiming to source items hard to find elsewhere and offer them at affordable prices. With some well-known and lesser-known brands, there's a great selection of dresses, tops, skirts and footwear. The owner urges customers to fight against the high street and join 'the start of the revolution for the individual!' ⓐ 13b Smith Street ❶ 01926 411140 ⓦ www.begorgeous.me ⓔ sales@begorgeous.me ⓛ 10.00–17.30 Mon–Sat

Castle Trains Children and adults alike will love the range of collectors' items and usable toys and games in this independent shop selling toy cars, model railways, kits and much more.
🅐 6 Smith Street 🕓 01926 497905 Ⓦ www.castletrains.com
🕔 09.00–17.30 Mon–Sat, 11.00–16.30 Sun & bank holidays

Corina Corina There aren't many shops where you can both buy and sell clothing, however Corina Corina take original vintage items – everything from 1940s tea dresses to 1970s leathers – and re-fashion these into unique garments. They also stock 'nearly new' designer labels and accessories, and provide a hire service for special occasions. 🅐 37 Smith Street 🕓 01926 400087 Ⓦ www.corinacorina.com 🅐 info@corinacorina.com
🕔 10.00–17.30 Mon–Sat

Eastgate Bookshop Looking just as an independent bookshop should, Eastgate's shelf-lined walls offer secondhand, antiquarian and modern books, with an emphasis on local history, military, children's books, literature and illustrated books.
🅐 11 Smith Street 🕓 01926 490607 🕔 09.30–17.30 Mon–Sat

Golden Monkey Tea Company With over 50 different types of tea, the Golden Monkey Tea Company is a loose tea merchant encouraging the drinking of tea as it was done long before the invention of the tea bag. Tea tins, tea-ware and gift boxes are there to accompany the hot stuff, alongside a special line of organic and Fairtrade chocolate. 🅐 64 Smith Street
🕓 01926 400544 Ⓦ www.goldenmonkeyteacompany.co.uk
🕔 10.00–17.30 Mon–Fri, 10.00–16.30 Sat

In Brief With a boudoir atmosphere, In Brief specialises in lingerie, corsets, hosiery, lounge wear and sports bras, as well as stocking a good range of swimwear all year round. It also offers a fitting service. ⓐ 66a Smith Street ⓣ 01926 411119 ⓦ www.inbriefboutique.com ⓛ 10.00–17.00 Mon–Wed, 10.00–17.30 Thur–Sat

The Quilter's Den The Quilter's Den shop and workshop caters for quilters and quilting fans alike with an array of colourful cottons, threads and silks. Regular quilting classes are also available and free patterns are often offered on the website. ⓐ 8 Smith Street ⓣ 01926 408247 ⓦ www.thequiltersden.co.uk ⓛ 09.30–17.00 Tues–Sat

🔺 Head to Smith Street for the best and most original of Warwick's shops

The Warwick Gallery Established in 1987 by local resident Peter Forde, The Warwick Gallery sells contemporary art. There are paintings of the local area and by local artists, including a few of Peter's own, as well as greetings cards, sculptures, wood, gifts, jewellery and tableware. ⓐ 14 Smith Street ⓣ 01926 495880 ⓦ www.art-is-a-tart.com ⓛ 09.30–18.00 Mon–Sat, 11.00–17.00 Sun

TAKING A BREAK

Chopsticks £ ❷ In a novel take on the 'all you can eat' buffet, Chopsticks has a £15 menu that allows you to eat all you can, but order each course individually. A good-value way of filling up for those with a large appetite. ⓐ 19 Smith Street ⓣ 01926 479188 ⓛ 17.30–22.30 Tues–Sun, closed Mon

Aqua Food and Mood ££ ❸ With a sister restaurant in Coventry, this Lebanese restaurant is heavy with an Eastern ambience that belies its Tudor exterior. Candlelit tables, rich silks and wall hangings and its own Bedouin Sheesha Garden all create a romantic vibe. There's a wide range of vegetarian meze-style nibbles as well as meat options. ⓐ 2–14 Jury Street ⓣ 01926 495491 ⓦ www.aqua-food-mood.co.uk/warwick ⓔ info@aqua-food-mood.co.uk ⓛ 17.30–22.30 Sun–Thur, 17.30–23.00 Fri & Sat

Giovanni's ££ ❹ A 25-year-old family-run favourite, Sicilian couple Giovanni and Silvana Castrofilippo serve authentic Italian cooking using fresh seasonal produce. Giovanni grows a lot of his own herbs and vegetables. The menu changes regularly with daily specials. Booking on weekends is advisable. ⓐ 15 Smith Street ⓣ 01926 494904 ⓒ 18.30–22.00 Mon–Sat, closed Sun

Lord Leycester Hotel ££ ❺ There are three options for food and refreshment at the Lord Leycester Hotel. The cosy, pub-like Stratford bar, the leather sofa-ed Oak Room and the Jesters Brasserie, which serves hearty breakfasts, lunch and dinner and is well known for its Sunday carvery. ⓐ Jury Street ⓣ 01926 491481 ⓦ www.lord-leycester.co.uk ⓔ reception@lord-leycester.co.uk

Piccolino's ££ ❻ Another family-run venue, Piccolino's also has a branch in Leamington Spa and does good-value pasta as well as fish and meat options. Popular with locals, it gets very busy at the weekends. You can watch your pizza being freshly baked in the large, specially built oven. ⓐ 31 Smith Street ⓣ 01926 491020 ⓦ www.ilpiccolinos.co.uk ⓒ 12.00–14.30 & 17.30–22.00 Mon–Fri, 12.00–23.30 Sat, 12.00–22.30 Sun

Warwick Spice ££ ❼ Boasting several accolades including the local press's 'best restaurant in town' recommendation, this award-winning Indian and Bangladeshi restaurant offers a good selection of favourite and lesser-known dishes. Baltis, tandooris and all the sundries are available, but the chef's special Jingha Masalla, with king prawns, cooked in the tandoori oven and with a tantalising combination of spices, is a real winner. Allow extra time when you order it. ⓐ 24 Smith Street ⓣ 01926 491736 ⓦ www.warwickspice.co.uk ⓒ 17.30–11.30 daily, including Christmas Day

Catalan £££ ❽ Bringing a little bit of Barcelona to the Warwick dining scene, Catalan is a fresh, tastefully decorated tapas bar and restaurant with a pretty back patio and good wine list. On weekends there is live music from local and not so local acts alike. There is also a good-value two-course 'Rustica' menu.
ⓐ 6 Jury Street ☏ 01926 498930 ⓦ www.cafecatalan.com
🕑 12.00–15.00 & 18.00–21.30 Mon–Thur, 12.00–15.00 & 18.00–22.00 Fri, 12.00–22.00 Sat, closed Sun

Robbie's £££ ❾ Smart dining in an unpretentious setting, Robbie's is a firm favourite with locals and visitors alike. Serving modern and traditional British and international fare such as Oven-Braised Lamb Henry and grilled fish of the day, there is also a good-value two-course menu and an extensive à la carte seafood menu. Save room for some of the inventive desserts.
ⓐ 74 Smith Street ☏ 01926 400470

🔺 Warm, welcoming and serving top-notch nosh

Ⓦ www.robbiesrestaurant.co.uk Ⓛ 11.00–22.00, closed Sun evenings unless booked

AFTER DARK

The Millwright Arms ⓰ It's worth making the walk down to Coten End to the Tudor-fronted Millwright Arms, first listed as a pub in 1880, which dates back to the 1600s and is said to have been used as a poorhouse. Home-cooked 'pub grub', beer, wines, teas and coffees are served in a collection of wooden-beamed rooms, with a large beer garden at the back. Ⓐ 69 Coten End Ⓣ 01926 496955 Ⓦ www.millwrightarms.co.uk Ⓛ 12.00–23.00 daily

New Bowling Green ⓫ Expect a warm welcome from licensee Leah Keyworth at the New Bowling Green, a 15th-century Tudor-style building just a short walk from the back of the castle. There are open fires, home-cooked meals, a range of real ales, wines and champagne and a beautiful walled beer garden, backing on to St Nicholas Park, in which you can play pétanque or boules. Ⓐ 13 St Nicholas Church Street Ⓣ 01926 411470 Ⓛ 11.30–23.00 Mon–Sat, 12.00–22.00 Sun

The Roebuck ⓬ Doing what Warwick does best in terms of traditional pub atmosphere, The Roebuck is a lovely old pub with lots of wood, warmth, wine and beer. It attracts a mixed crowd of locals and tourists, and the TV screen for football matches is discreet enough for those who don't care and good enough for those who do. Ⓐ 57 Smith Street Ⓣ 01926 494900 Ⓛ 11.30–23.00 daily

West of the castle

From Castle Street westwards, stretching to the boundaries of the old town at Warwick Racecourse, this area of Warwick has stunning examples of Georgian buildings, as well as some remaining medieval timber houses. Swan Street is the town's busiest shopping street, with an array of the type of independent retailers that Warwick is known for. Market Place, in the north of this area, has been a focal point of town life for centuries.

SIGHTS & ATTRACTIONS

Hill Close Gardens

These delightful Victorian gardens were originally owned by shopkeepers who, living above their businesses, had gardens attached to their properties. Rare examples of a common Victorian practice, some were used as allotments, some for ornamental purposes, they have survived only thanks to a local campaign and restoration project. The sixteen gardens are all differently decked out with some fine examples of Victorian fruit trees and flowers. Fascinating stories about local families who first tended the gardens are also told, and there are home-made cakes and other refreshments in the Hill Close Centre.
ⓐ Bread and Meat Close ⓣ 01926 493339
ⓦ www.hillclosegardens.com ⓛ 14.00–17.00 Fri & Sun, 11.00–17.00 Sat & bank holidays (Easter–end Oct)
ⓘ Admission charge

The Lord Leycester Hospital

Not a medical hospital but a charitable institution, this outstanding example of medieval timber housing sits next to the Norman gateway to the town and is still home to ex-servicemen and their spouses. **The Queen's Own Hussars Museum** (see page 69) is also housed here. The 12th-century Chantry Chapel forms part of the cluster of buildings around a picturesque courtyard; concealed behind is the small but enchanting **Master's Garden** (🕒 Easter–end Sept). The historic tea room perfects a visit. ⓐ 60 High Street ⓣ 01926 491422 ⓦ www.lordleycester.com ⓔ enquiries@lordleycester.com 🕒 10.00–17.00 Tues–Sun (summer); 10.00–16.30 Tues–Sun (winter)

🔺 *The charming Victorian Hill Close Gardens*

Market Place

The piazza-like square at the heart of Warwick has been a meeting point for centuries and still hosts the weekly Saturday market and

⬥ *Market Hall Museum offers a fun and educational family trip*

other events throughout the year. At the southern end of Market Place is the imposing Market Hall, built in 1670, which now houses the **Market Hall Museum** (see below).

Warwick Racecourse

Racing was introduced in Warwick after the great fire of 1694 in the hope of attracting wealthy investors to help with the rebuilding. The spectators' stand was built in 1809 and parts of this can still be seen today. Current races include both flat and jumps all year round. This was also the first course in the UK to include a jump race in its programme. ➋ Hampton Street ☎ 08445 793013 ⓦ www.warwickracecourse.co.uk ⏱ Race times vary, from midday onwards

CULTURE

Market Hall Museum

Make friends with the Warwickshire Bear (the centuries-old symbol for Warwick) at the Market Hall Museum, which now houses displays of local archaeology and natural history. Here you can learn more about the famous great fire of 1694 and also see some fascinating ancient artefacts, including a pair of Roman tweezers. ➋ Market Place ☎ 01926 412500 ⓔ museum@warwickshire.gov.uk ⏱ 10.00–17.00 Tues–Sat & bank holidays (year-round), 11.30–17.00 Sun (Apr–Sept only)

The Queen's Own Hussars Museum

One of the delights of a trip around The Lord Leycester Hospital (see page 67) is a visit to this museum, which offers an interesting history of the regiment right up until the present day, including social and military history. 60 High Street 01926 492035 www.qohmuseum.org.uk qohmuseum@qrh.org.uk 10.00–17.00 Tues–Sat (summer); 10.00–16.00 Tues–Sat (winter), closed Sun & Mon Admission charge

RETAIL THERAPY

SHOPS
Coco Rose Jeans, dresses, shoes, accessories, handbags and jewellery at this independent Swan Street shop stocking quirky independent, high-quality labels, many of which have a family business background. 3 Swan Street 01926 403020 www.cocorose.co.uk 10.00–17.30 Mon–Sat

Goldstraws Describing itself as a Creative Centre, Goldstraws stocks British manufacturers and Fairtrade makers of traditional toys, interesting gifts and local crafts. The first-floor **Joel's Gallery** is home to regular exhibitions of local artists and makers. 15 High Street 01926 410929 www.goldstraws. org.uk 10.00–17.00 Mon & Wed–Sat, 11.00–14.30 Sun, closed Tues

Present Days Established in 1977, this gift shop is packed floor to ceiling with cards, paper, bags, ribbon, homeware, pottery, stationery and anything anyone could possible need for a unique gift. The emphasis was on ethical and fair trade long before these became fashionable. 14 Swan Street

🕾 01926 494927 🅦 www.presentdays.co.uk 🕔 09.30–17.30
Mon–Sat, 11.00–16.00 Sun in Dec

Quinneys of Warwick (James Reeve Antiques) Established in the
1860s in Birmingham, the shop has been in its current location
for over forty years and is run by the present James Reeve and
his daughter. The beautiful Georgian building provides the
perfect backdrop for antique English furniture.
🅐 9 Church Street 🕾 01926 498113 🅦 www.jamesreeve
antiques.co.uk 🕔 09.30–17.00 Mon–Fri, 09.30–15.00 Sat

Russell Lane Russell Lane's jewellery shop stocks a wide range of
beautiful jewels and is a long-established purveyor of antique
and modern gems and precious objects. The glittering bracelets,
necklaces and rings in the windows are enticing enough, but
step inside for a closer look as well as a valuation service.
🅐 2 High Street 🕾 01926 494494 🅦 www.russell-lane.co.uk
🕔 09.30–17.00 Mon–Sat, closed Sun

Vintage Tucked into the corner of Market Place, Vintage has
15 stalls, selling good old fashioned bric-a-brac with crockery,
glassware and cutlery, as well as antiques and collectibles.
🅐 36 Market Place 🕾 01926 491527 🕔 10.00–17.00 Mon–Sat
(year-round), 11.30–16.30 Sun and bank holidays (summer only)

Warwick Antiques Centre A veritable warren of antiques and
collectables with up to 30 vendors under one roof. Furniture,
china, glassware, silver, toys, dolls and every conceivable kind
of collectible can be found. Those fond of a good browse could

disappear for days. ⓐ 22–24 High Street ⓣ 01926 491382
ⓛ 10.00–17.00 Mon–Sat, closed Sun

Warwick Books Set up in March 2004, Warwick Books is a
family-run bookshop stocking old and new books alike and
organising readings and book-based events in store. They pride
themselves on being able to access any book you like within
reason and ordering it in a lot faster than any of the large
chains. ⓐ 24 Market Place ⓣ 01926 499939
ⓦ www.warwickbooks.net ⓛ 09.00–17.30 Mon–Sat

▲ *Swan Street boasts some beautiful architecture*

MARKETS

In a town with a long-established market tradition, it's good to see market life survive and prosper, with a **weekly market** held every Saturday at Market Place (except Christmas and New Year's Day and when the Mop Fair takes place in October). Fruit and veg, clothing, toys, flowers, household goods and everything else you would expect from a typical market is on offer. With the terraces spilling out on to the streets there's a vibrant atmosphere. ⓐ Market Place 🕐 09.00–16.00 Sat

Every third Friday of the month there is also a genuine farmers' market, where you can buy fresh local produce directly from the growers and makers. This is a wonderful way to get a feel for the surrounding countryside and what grows there, with meat products, cheeses, fresh fruit, vegetables, pickles, pies and cakes all up for grabs. Go hungry so you can fill up as you walk round and don't forget to take something away for a picnic. ⓐ Market Place 🕐 09.00–14.00 third Friday of the month

There are also a number of **Continental**, **seasonal**, **garden** and **craft markets** held throughout the year, details of which are usually advertised around the town. Additional information is available from the tourist office (details in the Directory, page 93).

TAKING A BREAK

Smith's Fish-To-Go £ ⓭ Local businessman and chef Stefan Smith opened Smith's Fish-To-Go Bar in Brook Street after spotting a gap in the market, combining a traditional chippy with a fishmonger's and first-floor 1950s-American-style diner. Great for taking away and eating in alike. ⓐ 48 Brook Street

☎ 01926 492426 ⓦ www.smiths-fish-to-go.co.uk ⏰ 09.00–21.00
Tues–Sat, closed Sun & Mon

Wylie's Café £ ⑭ Seek out Wylie's, down the tiny Old Iron Yard,
for that perfect tea-room experience. ⓐ Old Iron Yard, off Market
Place ☎ 01926 490448 ⏰ Variable

Thomas Oken Tea Rooms £–££ ⑮ Oken House is one of
Warwick's oldest buildings and another Tudor survivor of the
great fire. The Thomas Oken Tea Rooms epitomise the English
tea room experience. Home-made lunches, cakes, puddings and
pies are all washed down with pots of tea. Traditional wicker
picnic hampers can be filled with your choice of treats to take
to the castle or parks and the cream teas always sell very well.

◔ *Mediterranean cool at Art and Wine*

Head upstairs for comfy sofas. Local ales and organic ciders are also available. ⓐ 20 Castle Street ⓣ 01926 499307 ⓦ www.thomasokentearooms.com ⓒ 10.00–17.30 Mon–Fri, 10.00–18.00 Sat & Sun

Art and Wine ££ ⓰ Gallery and fine wine store, Art and Wine manages a bit of everything with aplomb. The courtyard feels more Mediterranean than Midlands, the 400-year-old wine cellar, staircased hallway and upper gallery areas are all wonderful places to sit and admire works by local painters, as well as sip wine from £10 a bottle. ⓐ 8 High Street ⓣ 01926 496337 ⓦ www.artandwine.co.uk ⓔ info@artandwine.co.uk ⓒ 11.00–23.00 daily

Lane's Bar and Restaurant ££ ⓱ Local jeweller Russell Lane's restaurant attracts a sophisticated crowd of all ages with cocktails, champagne, lobster and English game specialities such as partridge. It's a lively and popular weekend hangout, with the emphasis firmly on local produce. Sunday lunch is a particular favourite. ⓐ 6 Castle Street ⓣ 01926 403030 ⓒ 12.00–14.30 & 18.00–22.00 Tues–Sat, 12.00–16.00 Sun, closed Mon

Totally Thai ££ ⓲ Another good Market Place location, Totally Thai has been operating for over ten years, with authentic and good-value Thai dishes. Ask for the special lunch menus and express menus if you want cheap, tasty food in a hurry, or linger longer over the full menu. ⓐ 16 Market Place ⓣ 01926 496187 ⓒ 12.00–14.30 & 18.00–23.00 Tues–Sat, 18.00–23.00 Mon, closed Sun

Dining at the Racecourse £££ ⑲ There are two dining options at the Racecourse. **1707** has been fashioned in a new, glass-fronted building opposite the finishing line, affording unrivalled views of the track as well as a private balcony. You keep your table for the day so it's a great place to set up camp. The **Chandler Champagne & Seafood Restaurant** needs no reservation and serves a range of champagnes and wines, with hot dishes available to warm you up in winter. ⓐ Hampton Street ① 08445 793013 ⓦ www.warwickracecourse.co.uk ① Race times vary

Tailors £££ ⑳ Tailors takes its name from this Market Place building's history, which, between 1858 and 1950, was a gentleman's outfitters. The fine dining menu includes roasted meats, fish and a good selection of vegetarian dishes, as well as traditional desserts. There's also a six-course taster menu and great-value two- and three-course menu options. ⓐ 22 Market Place ① 01926 410590 ⓦ www.tailorsrestaurant.co.uk ① 12.00–1400 & 18.30–21.30 Tues–Sat, closed Sun & Mon

AFTER DARK

Warwick nightlife mainly takes place in pubs and bar/restaurants. These are also often good places for taking a break earlier in the day, with some opening early enough to serve breakfast.

Alibi ㉑ Previously Rumours, this restaurant and wine bar aims to take advantage of its late licence and attract a select clientele with grills, a wine bar and cocktails, as well as regular live music slots on weekends. ⓐ 62 Market Place ⓣ 01926 493318 ⓛ 11.00–midnight Sun–Thur, 11.00–02.00 Fri & Sat

Merchants Wine Bar ㉒ Taking its name from the long history of merchants in town, this stylish winery has striking murals of Warwick and the castle throughout. The wine lists are extensive and the staff are always happy to recommended something different and interesting. They pride themselves on creating cocktails 'made to measure', depending on what the customers fancy. There is live music on Fridays and regular wine tastings. ⓐ Radio House, Swan Street ⓣ 01926 403833 ⓦ www.merchants warwick.co.uk ⓔ mail@merchantswarwick.co.uk ⓛ 12.00–late Mon–Sat, closed Sun

Rose & Crown ㉓ The popular Rose & Crown has developed into something of a gastro pub, with a strong emphasis on good-quality food from ethical producers at pub prices. Deli boards are a favourite and there are nice touches such as a bowl of Smarties served with coffee and tea. There are also five reasonably priced bedrooms for overnight bookings. ⓐ 30 Market Place ⓣ 01926 411117 ⓦ www.roseandcrown warwick.co.uk ⓛ 07.30–23.30 Mon–Sat, 08.00–23.00 Sun

Thomas Lloyd ㉔ If you're familiar with the Wetherspoon's chain, this cavernous public house will be as expected, with good-value beers, pub food and major sporting events and football matches shown on flatscreen TVs. The large terrace on Market Place makes it popular in the warmer months and, open late, it attracts a lively, beer-drinking crowd on weekends. ⓐ 3–7 Market Place ⓣ 01926 475690 ⓦ www.jdwetherspoon.co.uk ⓛ 07.00–midnight Sun–Thur, 07.00–01.00 Fri & Sat

The Tilted Wig ㉕ Sitting a few doors down from Thomas Lloyd, this listed Georgian building has housed a licensed premises on site since 1694. These days the Wig has a lively bar, a sports bar section, a restaurant area and B&B accommodation. The terrace is popular when weather permits. ⓐ 11 Market Place ⓣ 01926 410466 ⓦ www.thetiltedwig.co.uk ⓛ 12.00–23.00

▶ *The Royal Pump Rooms, Royal Leamington Spa*

OUT OF TOWN
trips

Royal Leamington Spa

Royal Leamington Spa owes its rapid expansion in the 19th century to the popularisation of 'curative' spa treatments. Elegant avenues, parks and Georgian mansions sprung up, and the town was granted its Royal prefix in 1838 by Queen Victoria.

GETTING THERE

It is a short drive from Warwick along the A445 (Coten End). Alternatively the number X18 bus takes the same route. Regular, direct trains from Warwick take four minutes. Riverside Walk is a pleasant 5.5-km (3½-mile) walk from Warwick.

SIGHTS & ATTRACTIONS

All Saints Church
Two of the town's founders, William Abbotts and Benjamin Satchwell, are buried in the graveyard of this large parish church. It is also the site of one of the mineral springs for which Leamington is so famous. ⓐ Victoria Terrace ⓣ 01926 429169 ⓦ www.allsaintsleamington.org.uk ⓛ Generally open daylight hours

Jephson Gardens
These stunning ornamental gardens were developed in the 1830s but descended into post-war decline. A vast refurbishment plan, adding a subtropical glasshouse and restaurant, has more than restored their former glory. ⓐ The Parade ⓛ 08.00–dusk daily

Royal Pump Rooms

Opening in 1814 and remodelled as a cultural centrepiece in the 1990s, **Art Gallery** showcases paintings from major British artists such as Paul Nash and Stanley Spencer. A **Local History Gallery**, telling the story of Leamington's growth as a spa town, is housed in the former Turkish Bath, and the old swimming pool is now the town library. ⓐ The Parade ❶ 01926 742700 ⓦ www.warwickdc.gov.uk/wdc/royalpumprooms ❸ 10.30–17.00 Tues, Wed, Fri & Sat, 13.30–20.00 Thur, 11.00–16.00 Sun & bank holidays, closed Mon

Town Hall

Built in 1884, this added to the expansion of the north side of the river or 'new town'. Outside is a statue of Queen Victoria, in thanks for bestowing the Royal prefix. ⓐ The Parade

◓ *Delight in Jephson Gardens when the weather is fine*

RETAIL THERAPY

Dolls Domain A delight for doll lovers, with a large range of dolls, dolls' houses and miniatures. Upstairs stocks over 2,000 jigsaws. ⓐ 1 Satchwell Court ⓣ 01926 314341 ⓦ www.dollsdomain.co.uk ⓛ 09.30–17.00 Mon–Sat, closed Sun, except six weeks prior to Christmas

Filthy But Gorgeous A sister store to The Warwick Gallery, focusing on contemporary designs by British artists, paintings, sculptures, crafts and cards. ⓐ 116 Regent Street ⓣ 01926 339966 ⓦ www.filthybutgorgeous.co.uk ⓛ 09.30–17.00 Mon–Sat, closed Sun

Lilac Rose Independent boutique offering eclectic gifts, jewellery, clothes and accessories. ⓐ 69 Regent Street ⓣ 01926 883800 ⓛ 10.00–17.30 Mon–Sat, 11.00–16.30 Sun

TAKING A BREAK

Bar Angeli £ Amidst the chains of Regent Court, this great Italian-city-style café has many atmospheric touches and serves excellent coffee and food. ⓐ Unit 5 Regent Court ⓣ 01926 887577 ⓛ 09.00–18.00 daily

Corleone Caffe £ A tiny but authentic Italian café with wonderful décor. Reasonable prices, decent food and tasty cakes. ⓐ 108 Regent Street ⓣ 01926 336444 ⓛ 09.00–18.00 Mon–Sat, 10.00–16.00 Sun

La Coppolla ££ Decorated with fruit and veg and murals, this has a good Italian menu and two floors of busy tables. ➍ 86 Regent Street ➊ 01926 888873 ➌ www.lacoppola.co.uk ➍ 12.00–22.00 daily

Mallory Court Hotel Dining Room £££ Warwickshire's only Michelin-starred restaurant, the Dining Room is an essential treat for award-winning cuisine, wood-panelled elegance and countryside views. There is also a great brasserie. ➍ Harbury Lane ➊ 01926 330214 ➌ www.mallory.co.uk ➍ reception@mallory.co.uk ➍ 18.30–21.00 daily ➊ Reservation necessary

AFTER DARK

Assembly This venue is where all the major artists and bands who come to the area perform. There are also weekend club nights. ➍ Spencer Street ➊ 01926 523001 ➌ www.leamingtonassembly.com ➍ Various – dependent on act. Club nights: 21.00–02.00 Fri & Sat

Saint Bar Styling itself as 'an ultra-chic hideaway', this underground club has cocktails, cushions and an outdoor terrace. ➍ 40 Warwick Street ➊ 01926 422550 ➌ www.saintbar.net ➍ 12.00–24.00 Mon, 12.00–02.00 Tues & Wed, 12.00–03.00 Thur–Sat, 12.00–01.00 Sun

Smack A haunt of students and locals alike, Smack has a slick interior and attracts well-known DJs. ➍ 5–9 Tavistock Street ➊ 01926 422223 ➌ www.trysmack.co.uk ➍ 22.30–03.00 Tues, 23.00–03.00 Thur & Fri, 23.00–04.00 Sat

Stratford-upon-Avon

At first sight Stratford-upon-Avon is all about Shakespeare, and indeed much of the town is given over to celebrating the world's best-known playwright. It is also a hotbed of performing arts, with history oozing out of every street.

GETTING THERE

From Warwick it's just over 13 km (8 miles) along the A429 and the A46. Direct trains take 25–30 minutes. The No 16 Stagecoach bus service also runs from Warwick to Stratford.

SIGHTS & ATTRACTIONS

Stratford boasts five houses with strong links to Shakespeare, which give a fascinating insight into Tudor homes and lifestyles. Information is available from **The Shakespeare Birthplace Trust**. ⓐ Henley Street ⓣ 01789 204016 ⓦ www.shakespeare.org.uk

Anne Hathaway's Cottage
Parts of Anne Hathaway's gingerbread-like cottage and idyllic garden, before she became Mrs Shakespeare in 1582, date back to the mid-1400s. ⓐ Cottage Lane, Shottery ⓛ 09.00–17.00 daily (Apr–Oct); 10.00–16.00 (Nov–Mar) ⓘ Admission charge

Hall's Croft
An outstanding house, once home to Shakespeare's eldest daughter. It includes 16th- and 17th-century furnishings, a tea

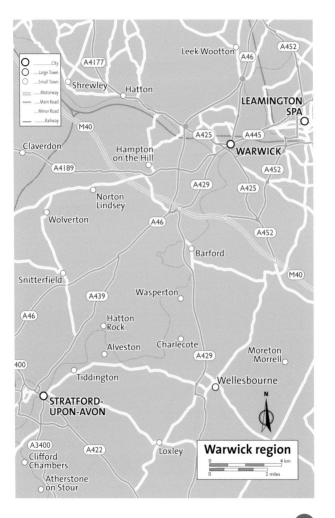

room and a charming garden. ⓐ Old Town ⓛ 10.00–17.00 daily
(Apr–Oct); 11.00–16.00 (Nov–Mar) ⓘ Admission charge

Mary Arden's House
Three miles outside town, the childhood home of Shakespeare's
mother hosts the **Shakespeare Countryside Museum** and two
historic farms. ⓐ Station Road, Wilmcote ⓛ 09.00–17.00 daily
(Apr–Oct); 10.00–16.00 (Nov–Mar) ⓘ Admission charge

Nash's House & New Place
A historic building and exhibition, this is where Shakespeare
once lived. ⓐ Henley Street ⓛ 10.00–17.00 daily (Apr–Oct); 11.00–
16.00 (Nov–Mar) ⓘ Admission charge

Shakespeare's birthplace
This is where the story began: in 1564 in a half-timbered house
on Henley Street. There is an exhibition of the dramatist's life,

⬢ Anne Hathaway's impossibly charming cottage

period furnishings and a pretty garden. ⓐ Henley Street
🕘 09.00–17.00 daily (Apr–Oct); 10.00–16.00 (Nov–Mar)
🛈 Admission charge

CULTURE

The Falstaff Experience

In a 16th-century barn, The Falstaff Experience's 'Tudor World' re-
enacts tales of Tudor Stratford and England. ⓐ 40 Sheep Street
📞 01789 298070 🌐 www.falstaffexperience.co.uk 🕘 10.30–17.30
(may vary) 🛈 Admission charge

The Royal Shakespeare Company

The Royal Shakespeare Theatre Company is unsurpassable. A
visit to Stratford is not complete without seeing one of their
performances. ⓐ Waterside 📞 0844 800 1114 🌐 www.rsc.org.uk

Shakespeare Centre Library

Founded in the late 1800s, the library holds original editions of
Shakespeare plays and some of the earliest printed books in
England. ⓐ Henley Street 📞 01789 204016 🌐 www.shakespeare.
org.uk 🕘 10.00–17.00 Mon–Fri, 09.30–12.30 Sat, closed Sun

RETAIL THERAPY

The Chaucer Head Bookshop A charming bookshop stocking
over 12,000 secondhand books on a range of subjects.
ⓐ 21 Chapel Street 📞 01789 415691 🌐 www.chaucerhead.com
🕘 10.00–17.30 Mon–Sat, closed Sun

Love Handmade Beautiful contemporary jewellery by designer Lora Leedham. ⓐ 8 The Minories, Henley Street ⓦ www.loraleedham.co.uk ⓛ 10.00–17.30 Mon–Sat, closed Sun

TAKING A BREAK

The Dirty Duck Day or night, the theatre folk's favourite 15th-century pub is an essential stop on any trip to Stratford. ⓐ Waterside ① 01789 297312 ⓦ www.dirtyduck-pub-stratford-upon-avon.co.uk ⓛ 11.00–23.00 daily

Hathaway's Tea Room Clotted cream, jam, tea and traditional nibbles at this quaint, antique-filled tea room. ⓐ 19 High Street ① 01789 292404 ⓛ 09.00–17.00 Mon–Sun

Lamb's Cosily appointed fine dining. ⓐ 12 Sheep Street ① 01789 292554 ⓦ www.lambsrestaurant.co.uk ⓛ 11.00–14.00 & 18.00–21.00 Mon–Thur, 11.00–14.00 & 18.00–22.00 Fri & Sat, 12.00–14.00, 18.00–21.00 Sun

Old Thatch Tavern Good beer and great food. ⓐ 23 Greenhill Street ① 01789 295216 ⓛ 11.00–23.00 daily

The White Swan Drink, dine and/or sleep in a five-hundred-year-old inn, said once to have been the bakery frequented by Shakespeare. ⓐ Rother Street ① 01789 297022 ⓦ www.pebblehotels.com ⓛ 11.00–23.00 daily

---

▶ *Follow where your feet lead in this compact and easily navigable town*

PRACTICAL
information

Directory

GETTING THERE

With its central location, Warwick is relatively easy to get to from all corners of England and very close to Birmingham and Coventry. It is linked to them by main motorway and A-road routes and it is also a straightforward drive from London of 125 km (78 miles).

By air

Birmingham International Airport (☎ 0844 576 6000 ⓦ www.birminghamairport.co.uk) operates flights to and from many UK and European destinations and to some further afield. Airlines include British Airways, Etihad, Flybe, Ryanair and Thomas Cook.

It is just over 27 km (17 miles), and a 30-minute drive from the airport to Warwick town centre. Car hire and taxis are readily available. Follow the A452 and then the A4177.

Many people are aware that air travel emits CO_2, which contributes to climate change. You may be interested in the possibility of lessening the environmental impact of your flight through the charity **Climate Care** (ⓦ www.jpmorgan climatecare.com), which offsets your CO_2 by funding environmental projects around the world.

By car

The M40 is the best main route if you are coming from the south or southwest of London and the M1 is best from the southeast of London, or from the east or north. From the north follow signs south towards Birmingham. On the M1, after passing Birmingham you will start to see signs for Coventry and Rugby.

By train

Again its central location makes Warwick easily accessible by train. Regular direct trains from London take an hour and a half. Direct services from Birmingham Snow Hill take around 42 minutes. To book in advance and enquire about train times, contact **National Rail Enquiries** (ⓣ 08457 484950 ⓦ www.nationalrail.co.uk). You can also try the **Trainline** (ⓦ www.thetrainline.com).

From Birmingham International Airport you have two options – to change at Birmingham Snow Hill or at Leamington Spa: both have direct services with a total journey time of about 50 minutes.

By coach

Warwick's main bus station is on Bowling Green Street and is served by coaches from London, Birmingham, Birmingham International, Oxford, Coventry and other key UK cities. Coaches are slower than trains but do tend to be cheaper. To contact **National Express** coach services for advice and tickets call the dedicated booking line (ⓣ 08717 818178 ⓦ www.nationalexpress.com).

GETTING AROUND

As it is a compact town, the best way to get around Warwick is on foot. There are local buses but these are mainly to get out of town or to residential areas on the outskirts. A car is great for seeing the surrounding countryside and villages. Car-hire outlets can be found at the airport or in town (see page 38).

Local taxi firms are available:

Castle Cars ☎ 01926 494989
Gold Star Taxis ☎ 01926 495000
Warwick Taxis ☎ 01926 499966

There is also a taxi rank in Market Square and there are usually some taxis for hire outside Warwick Station.

HEALTH, SAFETY & CRIME

Warwick has a lower-than-national-average crime rate and overall it is a very safe town. When walking home after dark the same rules apply as anywhere and it is advisable to keep an eye on personal belongings in busy, tourist-centred locations.

In a health emergency, dial 999 or 112. A full A&E service is provided at **Warwick Hospital** (ⓐ Lakin Road ☎ 01926 495321 ⓦ www.warwickhospital.nhs.uk). A Minor Injuries Unit operates at **Stratford-upon-Avon Hospital** (ⓐ Arden Street ☎ 01789 205831).

OPENING HOURS

Warwick has standard opening hours, with most shops opening around 10.00 and closing around 17.00. As in other small towns across the UK, many close on Sundays, except in the run-up to Christmas. Restaurants and pubs will also often close after lunchtime and reopen for the evening. Warwick is not a late-night town: most pubs stay open to 23.00 or midnight and there are only one or two later nightspots.

TOILETS

Public toilets can be found in Pageant Garden, Market Square and St Nicholas Park.

CHILDREN

Warwick is a wonderful place to take children, mainly because the castle is very well set up to entertain them. As well as the children's facilities in the castle, there are also extensive playgrounds and activities in St Nicholas Park (see page 30).

TRAVELLERS WITH DISABILITIES

Although built on a hill, the centre of town is mainly flat and fine for wheelchairs. Unfortunately, there are small doorways, tight corners and steep stairs in some of the listed buildings and in parts of the castle. Public toilets in Pageant Garden, Market Square and St Nicholas Park all have facilities for disabled, with a RADAR key available from the tourist office during opening hours.

There is no charge for drivers who display a disabled badge in any of the council-run car parks, unlimited parking on single yellow lines (providing you do not cause an obstruction) and two hours' free parking allowed on double yellow lines.

FURTHER INFORMATION

The Tourist Information Centre, housed in the old Court House, is a pleasure to visit in itself, with its high ceilings and wide corridors. Staff are very helpful and there is a good range of information, leaflets, maps and more available on Warwick and the wider county. The website is also a valuable resource of information, including history, culture, shopping guides and maps. ⓐ The Court House, Jury Street ⓣ 01926 492212 ⓦ www.visitwarwick.co.uk ⓔ info@visitwarwick.co.uk ⓛ 09.30–16.30 Mon–Fri, 10.00–16.30 Sat, 10.00–15.30 Sun

ACKNOWLEDGEMENTS
The photographs in this book were taken by Paul Walters for Thomas Cook Publishing, to whom the copyright belongs.

Project editor: Kate Taylor
Copy editor: Penny Isaac
Layout: Trevor Double
Proofreaders: Ting Baker & Angela Karakus
Indexer: Mary Purton

AUTHOR BIOGRAPHY
A travel writer, presenter and journalist, Lisa Francesca Nand studied in Warwickshire. She has been published widely in the national press, presents online travel videos and is a regular expert travel guest on national radio and television. With a passion for architectural history she loves Warwick's medieval past and can often be found in one of its many tea rooms.

Send your thoughts to
books@thomascook.com

- Found a great bar, club, shop or must-see sight that we don't feature?
- Like to tip us off about any information that needs a little updating?
- Want to tell us what you love about this handy little guidebook and more importantly how we can make it even handier?

Then here's your chance to tell all! Send us ideas, discoveries and recommendations today and then look out for your valuable input in the next edition of this title.

Email the above address (stating the title) or write to:
pocket guides Series Editor, Thomas Cook Publishing, PO Box 227, Coningsby Road, Peterborough PE3 8SB, UK.